Now yo...
flute sol...
recorded arrangements

jazz

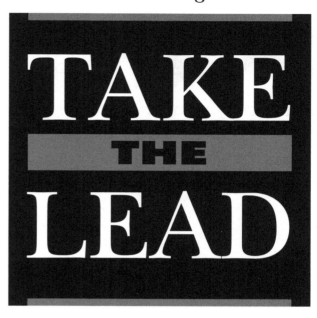

TAKE
THE
LEAD

flute

IMP

International
MUSIC
Publications

International Music Publications Limited
Griffin House 161 Hammersmith Road London W6 8BS England

Series Editor: Sadie Cook

Editorial, production and recording: Artemis Music Limited
Design and production: Space DPS Limited

Published 1999

International MUSIC Publications

© International Music Publications Limited
Griffin House 161 Hammersmith Road London W6 8BS England

IMP

International Music Publications Limited

England: Griffin House
161 Hammersmith Road
London W6 8BS

Germany: Marstallstr. 8
D-80539 München

Denmark: Danmusik
Vognmagergade 7
DK1120 Copenhagen K

Carisch

Italy: Via Campania 12
20098 San Giuliano Milanese
Milano

Spain: Magallanes 25
28015 Madrid

France: 20 Rue de la Ville-l'Eveque
75008 Paris

flute

TAKE THE LEAD

In the Book...

On the CD...

Demonstration

Backing

Birdland

Music by
Josef Zawinul

Desafinado

Demonstration Backing

Words by Newton Ferriera de Mendonca
Music by Antonio Carlos Jobim

Moderate Bossa Nova

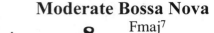

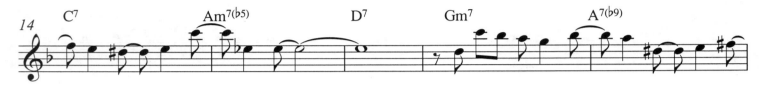

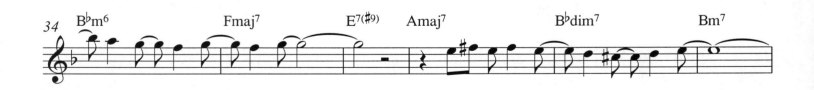

Don't Get Around Much Anymore

Music by Duke Ellington

Fascinating Rhythm

Music and Lyrics by
George Gershwin and Ira Gershwin

Misty

Music by Erroll Garner

Demonstration

Backing

My Funny Valentine

Music by Richard Rodgers

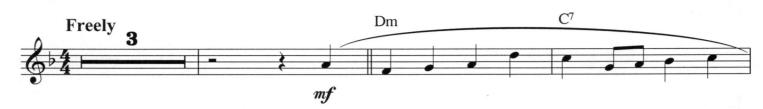

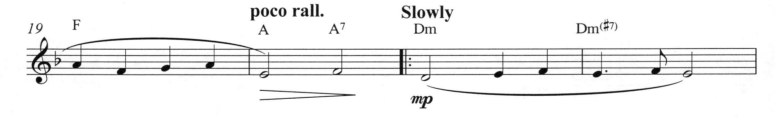

Demonstration

Backing

One O'Clock Jump

Music by Count Basie

Summertime

Music and Lyrics by George Gershwin,
Du Bose and Dorothy Heyward and Ira Gershwin

Demonstration

Backing

Reproduced and printed by
Halstan & Co. Ltd., Amersham, Bucks., England

You can be the featured soloist with
TAKE THE LEAD

Collect these titles, each with demonstration and full backing tracks on CD.

90s Hits	Movie Hits	TV Themes	Christmas Songs	The Blues Brothers
The Air That I Breathe (Simply Red)	**Because You Loved Me** (Up Close And Personal)	**Coronation Street**	**The Christmas Song** (Chestnuts Roasting On An Open Fire)	**She Caught The Katy And Left Me A Mule To Ride**
Angels (Robbie Williams)	**Blue Monday** (The Wedding Singer)	**I'll Be There For You** (theme from *Friends*)	**Frosty The Snowman**	**Gimme Some Lovin'**
How Do I Live (LeAnn Rimes)	**(Everything I Do) I Do It For You** (Robin Hood: Prince Of Thieves)	**Match Of The Day**	**Have Yourself A Merry Little Christmas**	**Shake A Tail Feather**
I Don't Want To Miss A Thing (Aerosmith)	**I Don't Want To Miss A Thing** (Armageddon)	**(Meet) The Flintstones**	**Little Donkey**	**Everybody Needs Somebody To Love**
I'll Be There For You (The Rembrandts)	**I Will Always Love You** (The Bodyguard)	**Men Behaving Badly**	**Rudolph The Red-Nosed Reindeer**	**The Old Landmark**
My Heart Will Go On (Celine Dion)	**Star Wars (Main Title)** (Star Wars)	**Peak Practice**		**Think**
Something About The Way You Look Tonight (Elton John)	**The Wind Beneath My Wings** (Beaches)	**The Simpsons**	**Santa Claus Is Comin' To Town**	**Minnie The Moocher**
Frozen (Madonna)	**You Can Leave Your Hat On** (The Full Monty)	**The X-Files**	**Sleigh Ride**	**Sweet Home Chicago**
			Winter Wonderland	
Order ref: 6725A – Flute	Order ref: 6908A – Flute	Order ref: 7003A – Flute	Order ref: 7022A – Flute	Order ref: 7079A - Flute
Order ref: 6726A – Clarinet	Order ref: 6909A – Clarinet	Order ref: 7004A – Clarinet	Order ref: 7023A – Clarinet	Order ref: 7080A - Clarinet
Order ref: 6727A – Alto Saxophone	Order ref: 6910A – Alto Saxophone	Order ref: 7005A – Alto Saxophone	Order ref: 7024A – Alto Saxophone	Order ref: 7081A - Alto Saxophone
Order ref: 6728A – Violin	Order ref: 6911A –Tenor Saxophone	Order ref: 7006A – Violin	Order ref: 7025A – Violin	Order ref: 7082A - Tenor Saxophone
	Order ref: 6912A – Violin		Order ref: 7026A – Piano	Order ref: 7083A - Trumpet
			Order ref: 7027A – Drums	Order ref: 7084A - Violin

TAKE THE LEAD

on these jazz classics

Birdland

Desafinado

Don't Get Around Much Anymore

Fascinating Rhythm

Misty

My Funny Valentine

One O'Clock Jump

Summertime

On The CD:
full backing tracks, professionally arranged and recorded
full demonstration recordings to help you learn the songs

In The Book:
carefully selected and edited flute arrangements with chord symbols in concert pitch

Take The Lead is an integrated series for Flute, Clarinet, Alto Sax, Tenor Sax, Trumpet, Violin, Piano and Drums. In each edition all the songs are in the same concert pitch key, so the different instruments can play together.

All accompanying chord symbols are in concert pitch for use by piano or guitar.

International MUSIC Publications

International Music Publications Limited
Griffin House 161 Hammersmith Road London W6 8BS England

Order ref: 7172A

ISBN 185909790-1

9 781859 097908 >

TRINITY GUILDHALL

Piano
Grade 5

Pieces & Exercises
for Trinity Guildhall examinations

2012–2014

Contents

Alternative pieces for this grade

All pieces in this volume have been edited with regard to current concepts of performance practice. Fingering, dynamics, articulation and pedalling have been suggested to assist candidates and their teachers in developing their own interpretations. Markings in square brackets are editorial.

Recommended metronome markings are given as a useful, but not definitive, performance guide for all pieces.

Repeats of more than a few bars should be omitted in the examination unless otherwise instructed in the syllabus or in this Trinity music book, but all *da capo* and *dal segno* instructions should be observed.

Every effort has been made to trace and acknowledge the copyright owners. If any right has been omitted or if any detail is incorrect, Trinity College London apologises and will rectify this in any subsequent reprints following notification.

Trinity College London would like to thank John Kember, Pamela Lidiard, Michael Round, Peter Wild and John York for their work on this series.

Music typeset by Moira Roach and New Notations London.

Important

Candidates and teachers must refer to the Information & Regulations booklet (www.trinityguildhall.co.uk/essentialinformation) for all examination requirements and regulations. Syllabuses and further information can be obtained from your Trinity Guildhall Centre Representative or Trinity's London office.